HIP
HOTELS
NEW YORK

HERBERT YPMA

HIP
HOTELS
NEW YORK

with 264 illustrations, 225 in color

Thames & Hudson

contents

what is HIP?

Travel has changed. No corner of the world is unfamiliar anymore; globetrotting has become decidedly more democratic; cut-price air fares make almost any destination possible; and the easing of border bureaucracy has undoubtedly made things less of a hurdle.

What this means is that we are now free to pursue experiences on a more individual level; to seek out destinations that strike a personal note in terms of architecture, location, ambience and design – destinations that make us think, 'Now that's my kind of place.'

And that, from the very beginning, has been the point of HIP HOTELS; to find and share unique, authentic, inspiring places that will make you simply want to 'pack a bag and go'. And you can go secure in the knowledge that there have been no shortcuts taken. Each hotel featured is one that I have stayed in myself and photographed. That's your assurance and guarantee that all the hotels in this book are truly **H**ighly **I**ndividual **P**laces.

Herbert Ypma

introduction

I grew up in New York – sort of. For ten years my father was a professor at Columbia University, but we lived upstate, not downtown. Every day he drove down the Palisades Parkway and across the George Washington Bridge, and although we lived in the country, we went to Manhattan every chance we had. Only towards the end of our decade-long tenure did my parents move to a little place in Greenwich Village. It was the best time they had in ten years. Much later, my father confessed to me, 'If I had known how much fun it was to live in the city, we would have done so from the very beginning.' And that is the story of New York. It's not pretty, it's not Paris, it's not full of parks and greenery and polite people, but it's got something, and that something gets almost anyone who steps foot in this fast-moving, fast-talking, hard-working metropolis.

lower east side

The Lower East Side was once an infamous part of Manhattan. The first tenement buildings in the city were constructed here in the 1830s, to house Irish immigrants. Although 'house' is probably a rich description, more like 'container' (tenement comes from the Latin *tenere*, or 'to hold'). History refers to these brick tenements ribbed with black fire escapes as immigrant housing, but they were little more than warehouses stuffed with dirt-poor refugees escaping everything from the Irish potato famine to the Jewish pogroms of Eastern Europe. Families were forced to live in abysmal conditions, with no running water or sanitation, and sometimes up to fourteen families were lodged in a single house. So dire was this stretch of New York that for a while, in the mid-1800s, it ranked as the most densely settled area on the planet, with 240,000 people resident per square mile. With a high infant mortality rate and cholera out of control, it was the setting for

legendary tales of infamy as depicted in Scorsese's *Gangs of New York*. Millions of immigrants found their way to the working class headquarters of New York: Irish and Germans in the 1840s and 1850s, Italians, Jews, Eastern Europeans and Chinese from the 1870s to the 1930s, Afro-Americans and Puerto Ricans after World War II, and Latin Americans, Asians and Russians in the 1980s and mid-1990s. And if it were not for the efforts of reformers such as Jacob Riis, a journalist whose life's mission was to photograph and write about these abysmal conditions, things would not have changed. Gradually, the standard of living improved and the area began to thin out. More recently, it has changed beyond recognition due to a different style of refugee – the former residents of SoHo in search of the edge and low prices: it seems almost every week another hip restaurant or bar pops up in between a Chinese tailor and a Jewish deli.

hotel on rivington

Situated bang in the middle of the Lower East Side, Hotel on Rivington is a study in contrast; a shiny glass and steel tower in a neighbourhood of dilapidated tenement buildings that once housed the highest density of immigrants in the world.

One of the last 'hoods' of Manhattan to slowly relent to the constantly shifting property market that is always in search of more affordable space, the Lower East Side differs from SoHo, TriBeCa, the Meatpacking District and Chelsea because there are no warehouses or industrial buildings – only rows of skinny, five and six storey brick buildings scarred by steel fire escapes on top of a never-ending series of fifteen-foot-wide shop fronts.

The limitation of the architecture is an assurance, in a way, that there will never be too many million dollar restaurants or cavernous clubs in the area. The same limitation applies to the prospect of a hotel. Nevertheless, in 2001, on the day after 9/11, Paul Stallings, one of the first property developers to grasp the neighbourhood's potential, made the bold commitment to build one from scratch. The idea was to create something not so much to 'blend in' as to 'fit in'.

A team was found to come up with a creative programme that would mirror the street cred that defined the area. Dutch *enfant terrible* Marcel Wanders worked on the public spaces and French designer India Mahdavi created the guestrooms. Both were inspired choices: India Mahdavi has made a name worldwide with timeless yet funky yet feminine furniture, while Marcel Wanders has proven, not without controversy, that removing the bourgeois concept of good taste is one of the only ways open to moving forward.

Four years later, and less than a year after opening, almost all of New York has now heard about the cave at the hotel entrance. What they probably don't know is that this is more than just a grotto. Not too long ago, Wanders created the now notorious egg vase by seeing how many eggs he could squeeze into a condom. The resulting rubber skin with egg bulges was cast as a vase, and Marcel's tunnel at Rivington is a piece of this vase design blown up to Jolly Green Giant size. The entrance is a hit, the Thor restaurant on the ground floor is consistently voted in New York's top 100 and the rooms are sumptuously spacious. But the real advantage of the hotel came as a surprise to everyone, including the owners. There had never been a tower in this area, so no one knew that the hotel would have such an amazing view: New York's famous skyline from a completely new perspective is a handy bonus for guest and proprietor alike.

address Hotel on Rivington, 107 Rivington Street, New York, NY 10002
tel +1 (212) 475 2600   **fax** +1 (212) 475 5959
e-mail info@hotelonrivington.com
room rates from $325

absolutely have to see
The Tenement Museum (108 Orchard Street). For a nation built on hope and promise, this is the flip side. A rare insight into the life of newly arrived immigrants. OK, you hate tours, but it's only an hour and it's the only way they'll let you see it.

must have lunch
Thor is the Viking God of the area, a thunderbolt of a restaurant enhanced by Wanders' wild wallpaper on the walls and ceilings and his outhouse in the middle of the space (just in case you're wondering, Thor is in the Hotel on Rivington).

A trapezoid-shaped parcel of land defined by Canal Street, Broadway, Barclay Street and the Hudson River, 'TriBeCa' was coined in the 1970s as an abbreviation of 'Triangle Below Canal'. Up until the early 1960s, this neighbourhood was a collection of warehouses built to accommodate mercantile exchanges, and the area was referred to as Washington Market. By the 1930s Washington Market had become the biggest wholesale market in Manhattan, but eventually moved to Hunts Point and predictably went into decline, leaving many warehouses and factories empty. A real estate entrepreneur created the name TriBeCa because he felt it would have far more appeal than the original name of Washington Market. And he was right. By the 1980s, renovation of the former industrial buildings started, driven by the search for New York's holy grail – more affordable space. In a sense, TriBeCa owes its subsequent boom to its close proximity to

SoHo and its skyrocketing prices. As in SoHo, the galleries and artists were the first to arrive (and leave), followed by a wave of residential loft conversions and an armada of restaurants and cafés. So far, TriBeCa has avoided the invasion of chain stores: the only retail venues are unique, like Bu and the Duck (children's clothing) and Urban Archaeology (interior design). TriBeCa has also hung on to some artistic street cred by the founding of the Tribeca Film Festival and Film Center, helped by the efforts of TriBeCa resident, Robert De Niro. Ironically, the area has returned to how it was before the markets moved in. In the late 1700s this neighbourhood was one of elegant brick houses and private parks. As architect Rem Koolhaas points out in his book *Delirious New York*, 'Because the city is an island, it has no option but to continue to reinvent itself', and so this part of Manhattan has returned to its residential roots, albeit with a trendier name.

tribeca grand hotel

From the outside, the Tribeca Grand looks like any of the odd collection of buildings that make up the cityscape of TriBeCa. It could be a warehouse or converted offices, and like most buildings in this oddly shaped area with its cobblestone streets, it is arranged at diverse geometric angles to other blocks. There's no large sign to give you any hint that on the inside this is a vast adult playground in the middle of an area that has become one of the most sought-after residential addresses in Manhattan.

With a restaurant on every other corner, more cafés than the Champs Elysées in Paris and some of the most individual boutiques of New York, TriBeCa is the perfect venue for life à la loft. The space and light afforded by converted mercantile buildings and the lifestyle of fashionable eating, drinking and shopping all in walking distance, blend so beautifully that this area has now become one of New York's most expensive neighbourhoods.

But TriBeCa also has one other feature often overlooked (until 9/11) – its proximity to Wall Street. To people working in New York's Financial District, the dream is to stay in TriBeCa and work on Wall Street, which is what many residents do. But this was not an option for out-of-towners until the Tribeca Grand came along.

Opened in May 2000, this hotel, the only one in TriBeCa, has managed to combine the qualities that the area was missing: namely capacity, location and a style in sympathy with the neighbourhood. With over two hundred rooms, the Tribeca Grand caters to plenty of suits headed for Wall Street, as well as to the more casual creative types and visitors attracted by the growing Tribeca Film Festival.

Surprisingly for such a large hotel, it has created an interior that is in keeping with the industrial spirit of the area, even though it's obvious that the hotel is newly built. Big industrial-style steel beams define the massive skylight in the central atrium, and although the very idea of an atrium can remind me of a Marriot, in this case it is executed in a style that's sufficiently commensurate with the visual profile of TriBeCa. In fact, the giant space known as the Church Lounge has become a popular destination in its own right. The Sanctum restaurant and Church Lounge bar are packed at night, and during the day this internal space has morphed into a favourite hangout for people with laptops who want to work while being part of the scene. On reflection, this huge open space with its muted earthy contemporary tones is exactly in step with the area. Space, light and style are what the Tribeca Grand delivers, just like the neighbourhood.

address Tribeca Grand Hotel, 2 Avenue of the Americas, New York, NY 10013
tel +1 (212) 519 6600   **fax** +1 (212) 519 6600
e-mail reservations@tribecagrand.com
room rates from $339

absolutely have to see
Tribeca Cinemas, the premier Manhattan art house and home of the Tribeca Film Festival, is a movie theatre on Varick Street which was bought by Robert De Niro and partners and reopened as an art house hosting screenings and film events.

must have lunch
Brunch at Bubby's (120 Hudson Street, +1 (212) 219 0666): a TriBeCa institution. Famous for its all-American food, it has a Norman Rockwell style interior, and fabulous pies from the Bubby's pie company. A great classic.

soho

Nothing to do with London's Soho, this area is another example of New York's fondness for welded abbreviations. SoHo in Manhattan terms is the shortened version of South of Houston (pronounced 'house-tun'). Once a commercial area distinguished by elegant warehouses sporting neoclassical refinement and detailing, SoHo lays claim to the first development of the cast-iron building technique. Strictly utilitarian in function, these warehouses nonetheless featured pillars, arches and other flourishes, made possible by the load-bearing nature of the cast-iron skeleton. Little did turn-of-the-century architects – intent on adding decoration to plain packing warehouses – realize they had created the twenty-first century's most desirable residential option: the loft. Although 'loft' tends to be a word applied these days to almost any empty interior with white walls and the odd bit of groovy designer furniture; the original context applied

to open spaces, unencumbered by walls or doors, with just the occasional cast-iron pillar. For artists these spaces were ideal, but for living they were tough; tough to find privacy and tough to heat. I have a friend whose father is an artist, and they lived the real bohemian version of loft life in SoHo long before anyone wearing black Japanese clothing ever ventured there. While her father was drinking with other artists in Fanelli's, she dreamed of a house with doors and walls and a real bedroom with curtains and frilly bits. The artists, including my friend's father, have long since gone, and SoHo has developed into one of the most active, 24/7 neighbourhoods in Manhattan, without a doubt one of the best places to shop and eat in New York. Alas the old SoHo is no more, but the neighbourhood is still far more contemporary in its thinking than the rest of Manhattan. If it has one thing in common with uptown New York though, it's the prices.

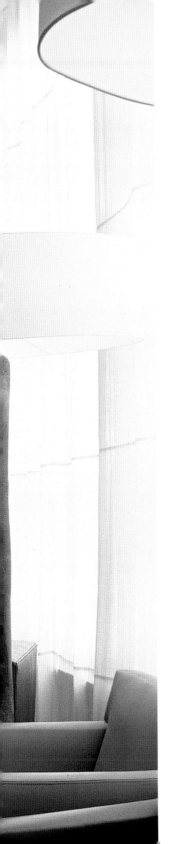

the mercer

SoHo is a unique neighbourhood in Manhattan because it's the only area without skyscrapers. The tallest buildings are a modest six storeys. Once upon a time these light-filled warehouses, with their acres of space, were inhabited almost exclusively by industry. Then, after a period of neglect and abandonment, they were discovered by artists, who moved in and transformed the buildings and the area too.

A decade ago André Balazs, hotel impresario and proprietor of LA's Chateau Marmont, acquired an imposing red-brick building on the corner of Prince and Mercer Streets, in the heart of trendy SoHo. By preserving the windows, the ceiling height and the proportions of the warehouse space, The Mercer is the first hotel to offer a taste of 'loft living', an urban signature that is completely original to New York City. The conventional notion of a hotel room has been abandoned. Instead every room feels like a loft, with plenty of space and natural light – exactly what attracted the community of artists who first gave this area its distinctive character.

A loft demands a design approach that enhances rather than fills the space. That is why Balazs chose to work with Parisian designer Christian Liaigre. The combination of handsome, pared-down furniture in African Wenge wood, neutrally toned textiles, simple lamps, dark wooden floors, pure white walls, crisp white linen, and a hint of lilac leather on elegant banquettes is exactly what was needed – a subtle, clean and classic approach that steers clear of furniture fashion. The design commitment to the loft experience continues with the bathrooms which are open to, and part of, the overall interior.

The Mercer Kitchen, a restaurant located in the basement of the building, creates the feel of eating in the kitchen, 'always the best setting for conversation among the best of friends,' according to Balazs. The ambience combined with the cuisine of chef Jean-Georges Vongerichten has made The Mercer Kitchen one of the most consistent restaurants in SoHo.

The matte-black crowd of ad agency staff, art directors, photographers and fashion people may have shunted out the artists, but SoHo still has an attitude you won't find on the Upper East Side. For Nathan Silver, author of *Lost New York*, 'if anything should stand forever as a radiant image of the essential New York, it ought to be these [SoHo's] commercial buildings.' Continually evolving in response to contemporary needs, they are 'the best and purest that New York has to offer'.

address The Mercer, 147 Mercer Street, New York, NY 10012
tel +1 (212) 966 6060   **fax** +1 (212) 965 3838
e-mail reservations@mercerhotel.com
room rates from $480

absolutely have to see
Prada Store (575 Broadway at Prince Street). It's fitting that in a neighbourhood disparagingly referred to as a shopping mall, a shop has replaced fashion as art. The SoHo Prada Store, designed by Dutch architect Rem Koolhaas, is exactly that: a challenging view of retail, even if few people are actually buying anything.

must have lunch
Saunter down the stairs to The Mercer Kitchen (+1 (212) 966 5454) which is still ranked as one of New York's top restaurants.

60 thompson

60 Thompson was created by the Pomeranc Group, a company that started out in the 1950s and expanded its real estate ventures to include a fat portfolio of airport hotels. Thompson was its first luxury project, but the experience of building and managing normal hotels was definitely not a disadvantage.

Ironically, given its ideal location on a rare quiet stretch right in the heart of SoHo, this project was originally meant to be uptown on the West Side, in the exact location of the Hudson Hotel in fact. The people at Pomeranc had set their hearts on this Upper West Side building only to discover, at the eleventh hour, that they had been outbid by Ian Schrager.

Feeling thoroughly dejected, Jason Pomeranc and his brothers took a cab down to have lunch at SoHo's Lucky Strike, and it was while they were dining that they noticed a 'for sale' sign on a rundown garage across the street. Not only was the location perfect, but it offered the opportunity to knock down and start from scratch – a plus for a real estate developer, not only because it makes a project cheaper and quicker, but also because it offers the chance to custom-design.

At thirteen storeys, 60 Thompson is one of the highest buildings in the area, and the planning stage was not without its hurdles. In order to secure permission to build high, New York property law dictated that Pomeranc and his brothers had to buy 'air rights' from all their neighbours. 'I own all the air on this block,' Jason Pomeranc now jokingly boasts. It no doubt helped, from a planning point of view, that the architect who designed the building, Stephen Jacobs, was a pioneer in turning SoHo and TriBeCa's industrial spaces into residential lofts.

For the interiors Pomeranc turned to Thomas O'Brien, head of Aero Studios, whose past work includes apartments for high-profile clients such as Giorgio Armani and Donna Karan. The interiors take their cue primarily from, oddly enough, an old photo of Burt Lancaster lounging on a very long couch at his home in Malibu. Hence the deep-buttoned velvet banquette in the lobby that stretches the entire length of the hotel.

Being one of the tallest buildings in SoHo also means there are great views from the hotel's rooftop, where the terrace bar has become a SoHo summer destination in its own right.

address 60 Thompson, 60 Thompson Street, New York, NY 10012
tel +1 (877) 431 0400 **fax** +1 (212) 431 0200
e-mail info@thompsonhotels.com
room rates from $539

absolutely have to see
Since retail is the new game in SoHo, why fight it? Take the opportunity to visit the kind of shops you don't find elsewhere in the United States, in particular Jack Spade on 56 Greene Street: New York's answer to Paul Smith.

must have lunch
Cipriani (376 West Broadway, +1 (212) 343 0999) with its authentic food and stylish interior is one of Manhattan's most popular Italian restaurants – quite an achievement considering New York's notoriously short restaurant attention span.

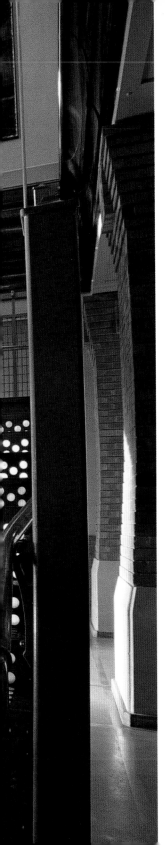

soho grand hotel

Unfazed by local objections, proprietor Emanuel Stern took a constructive attitude towards the obstacle of disapproval. He readily acknowledges that artists are the ones who come in and make an area attractive, while businessmen merely follow in their wake to capitalize on that. So to ensure that his approach was not seen as exploitative Stern made the smart commitment to root his hotel as much in the local community as possible.

In practice this meant employing a SoHo-based designer, working with SoHo-based artists and galleries, and drawing from the SoHo vernacular for the internal and the external architecture of the hotel. Stern interviewed fourteen designers before settling on William Sofield, ex-partner in SoHo's trend-setting Aero Design studios.

Sofield, whose former work includes creating many of the famously seductive room settings for Ralph Lauren Home, approached this project by blending the area's industrial background with the rich vocabulary of the local architecture. SoHo's famous loft buildings feature Victorian, Italianate, Oriental and even Egyptian-inspired embellishment and detailing. Thus the Egyptian columns, oriental lanterns and turn-of-the-century Arts and Crafts ornament that distinguish the Soho Grand's interior have a secure local precedent. But it may well have been the constraints placed on Sofield that inspired the true creativity of his scheme. A host of restrictions was put in the hotel's way. According to city ordinance, for instance, the ground floor was prohibited from being used because the area is, by legal definition, a flood plain – even though the swamp that prompted this legislation was filled in a century ago.

Thus the entrance is quite out of the ordinary, a bit like arriving in a subway station. This brutalist space – an empty cavern dominated by immense brick columns and a staircase of steel girders – serves as an anteroom to the main lobby and reception one floor above. It heightens the impact not just of the lobby, but also of the staircase, embedded with the glass bottle-bottoms traditionally used along SoHo sidewalks. The Soho Grand's design is gutsy, industrial and artistic, an apt metaphor for SoHo itself. In fact, even the locals who once opposed the hotel so vigorously now regularly drop in for lunch.

address Soho Grand Hotel, 310 West Broadway, New York, NY 10013
tel +1 (212) 965 3000   **fax** +1 (212) 965 3244
e-mail reservations@sohograND.com
room rates from $334

absolutely have to see
Visionaire (11 Mercer Street) is a shop that thinks it's a gallery and vice versa. One of the few art-related premises that has not decamped SoHo in favour of Chelsea, it is a handy place to buy a meaningful souvenir.

must have lunch
Honmura An (170 Mercer Street, +1 (212) 334 5253) is the recipient of the unheard-of honour of three stars from the *New York Times*. Who would have known there were soba noodle cognoscenti in Manhattan?

meatpacking district

Twenty years ago, unless you were a butcher or a debauched adventurer mesmerized by the prospect of unsafe sex in the underbelly of the city, this was not a part of town you were likely to visit. Home to more than 200 slaughterhouses, this was Manhattan's centre for wholesale meat. During the day, brawny men lugged bloody carcasses; at night it was the gutter of choice for cruising transsexual prostitutes and hardcore S&M clubs. The trucks – the large trailers left open at night for loading the next morning with meat – were infamous as handy containers for anonymous encounters, and gave new meaning to the notion of packing meat. And then there was the stench. As Hal Rubenstein, author of *I'll Eat Manhattan*, described it: 'Damn, it reeked. So slick was the river of beef tallow that in winter the street could easily have been varnished in ice, only to flow so pungently in summer that navigating the road promoted an exercise in breath control.'

Then in the 1990s the Meatpacking District evolved into New York's wild party destination, and the seedy reputation of the area only enhanced the edge of the new party scene. To put it in the most polite terms, the Meatpacking District was 'eccentric' and therein lies the very reason it has seen such a resurgence in interest. New Yorkers are drawn to treacherous forgotten corners, and it's the complete unlikeliness of this area as a prospect for gentrification that has made it so irresistible. Today, purists will tell you that the edge has gone: there are only a handful of meat warehouses still operating, and way too many bars and restaurants have taken their place. But then that's the nature of this city – New York is always on the move. For visitors it's a different story, the question is 'how much edge do you want?' And particularly in comparison to beautified European capitals, the Meatpacking District still has plenty of edge, and, if it helps … it still stinks.

soho house

The façade is small, the tiny reception is not even big enough to be called a lobby, and the text on the door is smaller than an Out to Lunch sign. It's the reverse of the 'Come In We Want to Impress You' lobby of hotels generated by famous designers. The message at Soho House is 'Go Away We Don't Want You … Unless You're A Member'. 'Charming,' you say, 'what kind of hotel is this?' And that's the point. Soho House is not a hotel, it's a private club – the hottest private club in New York – that happens to have a small hotel.

The rules are simple: if you're not a guest you cannot eat in the restaurant, swim in the pool, lunch on the roof, drink in the bar, watch a film in the private screening room, throw a party in the library or chill out in the Cowshed – the club's famous spa – unless you're a member. Two key words apply to Soho House; privacy, exclusivity and laid-back charm. Oops that's more than two, but you get the idea.

One thing it is not is stuffy. As a club, it has managed to attract the kind of people that normally never belong to clubs. Film directors, writers, artists, creative types in all fields make up the member roster, and yet Soho House is not painfully arty either. It has successfully struck a balance between being cosy and trendy, if there's such a thing. Part of the credit, without a doubt, goes to designer Ilse Crawford, whose great strength is that she wasn't a designer when she took on the job. She was a journalist, a magazine editor, who had shaped an entire publication in the mould of what she liked and what she didn't. She brought an editorial freedom to the interior of Soho House that goes beyond established notions of style.

Traditional, deep-buttoned chesterfields share the same space with Saarinen tables, Italian lamps and Danish design classics. The look, if it has to be defined as such, is a mix of laid-back modern and iconic antique, with the odd bit of 'Bling'. Unlike The Mercer, which gives you pared-down minimal loft spaces, Soho House gives you bohemian loft – big, baroque carved beds, egg-shaped tubs, French-style cupboards, consoles from the 1950s, 1960s lamps etc. But more important than how it looks is how it feels. Somehow it conjures the warmth and hospitality of a small, private British club in the most hyped-up area of Manhattan.

address Soho House, 29–35 Ninth Avenue, New York, NY 10014
tel +1 (212) 627 9800   **fax** +1 (212) 627 4766
e-mail reservations@sohohouseny.com
room rates from $445

absolutely have to see
They call it 'The White Cube' – an area of nearby Chelsea that houses the largest concentration of contemporary art galleries in the world.

must have lunch
Florent (+1 (212) 989 5779). Florent Morellet was a pioneer from Paris, enamoured with the eccentric side of New York and appalled by the yuppification of dining. He found an authentic diner at 69 Gansevoort Street and made it one of the most endearing uncomplicated places to eat good food in New York, 24/7.

hotel gansevoort

Too much is never enough. If this is your mantra, then Gansevoort is your hotel. Bigger than all the other buildings in the Meatpacking District, and often accused of not fitting in architecturally, it certainly does conform to the main reason most people come to this part of town; namely to eat and drink.

With all the different bars and lounges on the roof, the heavily booked new age Japanese restaurant Ono on the ground floor, the bamboo pavilion Chinese-inspired bar, and the day spa that turns into a subterranean lounge after hours, there's no shortage of entertainment on offer.

The elevator to the rooftop must log more miles each night than a yellow cab during rush hour. With a big swimming pool and a view of the setting sun over the Hudson River, it's not hard to understand why. This is a very Manhattan kind of bar, the kind of place you might expect to pop up in the next Woody Allen film. With four separate and different lounges, both inside and out, covering 5000 square feet of glass-enclosed space surrounded by the skyline of Manhattan, the Gansevoort has so thoroughly put its stamp on the idea of a rooftop playground that it has made it the signature of its expansion plans.

The Gansevoort hotels in Miami and Los Angeles are also planned around vast rooftop entertaining areas. The advantage for overnight guests is clear – you don't have far to travel to be part of the action. Just step in the elevator, press 'PH' for the penthouse roof, 'L' for the lobby or 'B' for the basement. The Gansevoort is not just a 'scene' but a collection of scenes. You don't ever need to venture out of the building to enjoy the hedonistic energy of Manhattan.

Even the uniforms of the bar staff have been coordinated to go with the nightlife: cocktail waitresses on the roof wear large Jackie O-style sunglasses and in the bamboo bar next to Ono the outfits are shiny Chinese red satin tops, white hot pants and big boots. By contrast, the rooms themselves are quite sedate. Decorated in shades of grey, with tasteful contemporary furniture, they are almost corporate in their avoidance of anything too risqué or trendy. But perhaps that was the intention – to provide a restrained repose from all the partying going on in the rest of the hotel. In any case, the average guest probably wouldn't even notice when they collapse on their bed, half-dressed, fully tanked. If you have lots of work to do, and want early morning starts, the Gansevoort may not be for you. On the other hand, you might live life according to Hemingway's famous quip: 'The true test of a man [or a woman] is the ability to work with a hangover.'

address Hotel Gansevoort, 18 Ninth Avenue (13th Street), New York, NY 10014
tel +1 (212) 206 6700   **fax** +1 (212) 255 5858
e-mail contact@hotelgansevoort.com
room rates from $395

absolutely have to see
The cutting-edge design stores Vitra (29 Ninth Avenue), Karkula (68 Gansevoort Street) and Lars Bolander (72 Gansevoort Street), combine interior style with exterior grit. But the sight really worth seeing is not yet complete – an old rail line converted into the world's first elevated park.

must have lunch or dinner
Spice Market at 403 West 13th Street (+1 (212) 675 2322) is Jacques Garcia's inventive take on Oriental Fusion Cuisine.

chelsea

Chelsea got its name from Captain Thomas Clarke who retired to this then rural area in 1750 and named it after Chelsea Royal Hospital, a home for retired soldiers in London. During the early 1800s, as the commercial and residential centre of New York moved further north, it was entirely predictable that this neighbourhood would enjoy the same gentrification as its counterpart on the east side of Fifth Avenue. Some town houses were built, but for no apparent reason, New York's uptown migration leapfrogged Chelsea. Industry moved in, residential tenants moved out, and the area began a downward slide until it became one of New York's less appealing neighbour-hoods, with its mix of sleazy tenements and dilapidated warehouses. Then, slowly, the area started to change as it almost always does in New York; by stealth. The gay community in neigh-bouring Greenwich Village began spilling into Chelsea, renovating town houses and reinventing

industrial spaces as bars, boutiques and brasseries. With the introduction of money and style into a neighbourhood that still had some edge, it was only a matter of time before the galleries arrived. And arrive they did, creating in a relatively short space of time the largest concentration of modern art galleries anywhere in the world. From the obscure and affordable, to the big names with six figures, it's all here in a square area so dense with white-walled galleries that it has earned the nickname 'The White Cube'. Still, despite recent beautification and the arrival of the art scene, Chelsea is still best remembered for its most infamous address, the Chelsea Hotel, where Sid Vicious killed his girlfriend before killing himself; where Arthur Miller checked in because he was sick of putting on a tie and jacket just to get his mail at the Plaza; and where rock stars and/or actors will decamp if they need to get themselves, or their careers, back on track.

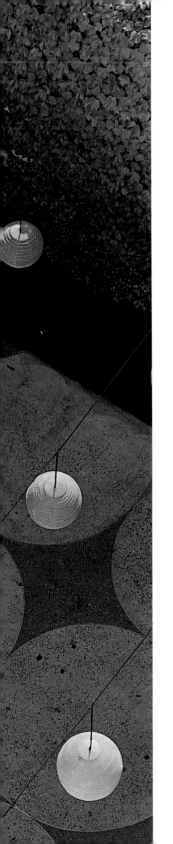

the maritime hotel

Of all the new hotels in New York, The Maritime Hotel would have to be the most architecturally distinctive; an imposing modernist rectangle with a gleaming white ceramic façade punctuated by more than 200 three-foot-wide portholes. Designed by New Orleans architect Albert C. Ledner as the headquarters for the National Maritime Union, it comes as no surprise that the building was completed in 1966 – a time when circles and curves were informing everything from André Courrèges dresses to Kubrick's *2001: A Space Odyssey*.

And it was this architecture that seduced impresarios Eric Goode and Sean MacPherson into reinventing the office building as a hotel. Charged by the complete originality of the building and the unusualness of the design, they tapped into their experience of creating New York nightlife hotspots such as Area, the Bowery Bar and the Park Restaurant (a converted taxi garage), and West Coast places such as Bar Marmont, Swingers and El Carmen in Los Angeles. The result is a hotel unlike any other in Manhattan, not only because of its porthole architecture but because it's a New York venue that offers as much outdoor space as indoor. As the owners will tell you, where else in Manhattan can you have breakfast outside on a sunny day, particularly without the shadows normally cast by New York skyscrapers? One of the problems with outdoor spaces in Manhattan is the shade and wind created by the concrete canyons. In Chelsea, The Maritime is the tallest building around, and thus light is not trying to squeeze past impossibly tall buildings. But the cleverest part of The Maritime Hotel is the impression that it has always been like this.

To stay true to the architecture the designers travelled extensively, checking out the work of other modern innovators such as Oscar Niemeyer in Brazil and Le Corbusier in France. A maritime theme prevails throughout: the guest rooms are kitted out like boat cabins, and although they are smallish, the precise use of space to squeeze in everything from a personal stereo system to a sizeable worktop make them very accommodating. The ship's cabin motif is reinforced by the huge portholes which in turn offer a view of the water. In the lobby, stylized murals repeat the marine theme, combined with furniture that is both retro and in some cases original. The balance that Goode and MacPherson achieved so well is the marriage of this marine theme with funky 1960s architecture without the sense that it is contrived.

address The Maritime Hotel, 363 West 16th Street, New York, NY 10011
tel +1 (212) 242 4300   **fax** +1 (212) 242 1188
e-mail james@themaritimehotel.com
room rates from $345

absolutely have to see
Dia Center for the Arts (535 West 22nd Street) is *the* place for installation art. These days no gallery is complete without a bookstore, and this follows the art installation theme, with a kaleidoscopic tiled floor by Cuban artist Jorge Pardo.

must have lunch
Check out Buddakan (75 Ninth Avenue, +1 (212) 989 6699), the latest big name, big budget restaurant to open in New York – Louis XV style chinoiserie meets Manhattan modernism from the design studio of Paris-based Christian Liaigre.

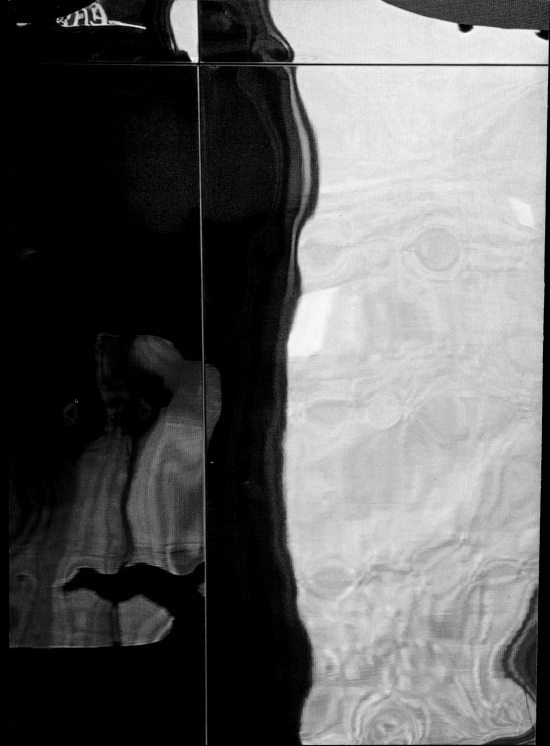

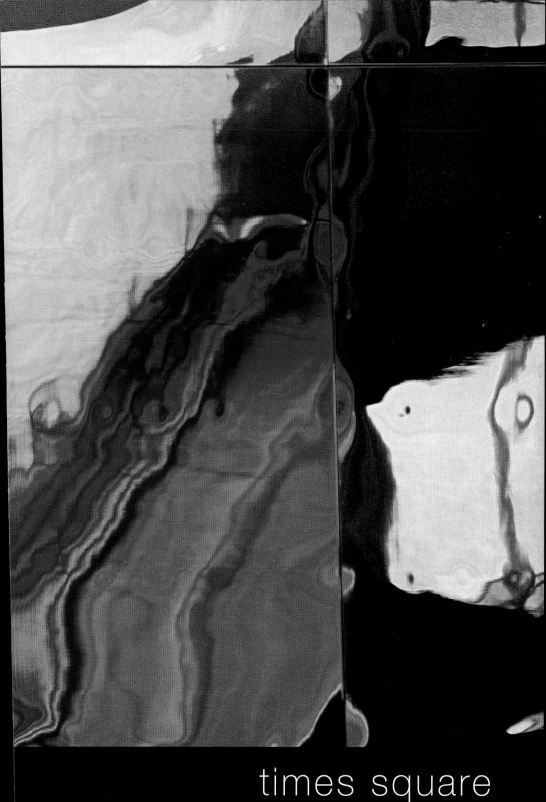

times square

In the 1920s it was known as the 'Great White Way' – a reference to its bright lights. Back then the neon was limited to theatres but there were so many of them (about 100) that they lit up a substantial stretch of Broadway from 56th Street down to 42nd Street. This triangle, where Seventh Avenue and Broadway converge, was New York's theatre district, and from 1927 until 1928, a record 264 shows were produced there. But the area took a big knock from the stock market crash of 1929. Many theatres closed, and others were converted into cinemas that showed risqué erotic films. World War II only made matters worse, and again, the demand for theatres plummeted in direct proportion to the demand for more adult entertainment by troops on R&R. It was a slide into the seedier side of life whose rock bottom was immortalized in John Schlesinger's 1969 *Midnight Cowboy* – set almost entirely in and around Times Square.

Once known for its theatres, Times Square had become infamous for its adult cinemas, strip clubs and prostitutes: bright lights, big city to bright lights, sin city. Unsuspecting tourists looking for the Times Square made famous by the annual New Year's Eve gathering were in for a shock. But New York has a history of fighting back: the vice has moved further west and Times Square has a new identity, shaped by the arrival of a new generation of entertainment. The neon is bigger and badder than ever, thanks partially to a new city ordnance that makes it obligatory for buildings in this area to feature neon advertising. There's still far more to see than to do in Times Square, and the neon remains the area's drawcard. It brings to mind G. K. Chesterton's famous quote from 1922, 'What a glorious garden of wonder this would be, to anyone lucky enough to be unable to read.'

night hotel

The Night Hotel is dedicated to the dark side of the metropolis; to Manhattan after dark. To get in the right mood for this new nocturnally inspired addition to New York's hotel scene, get a copy of *Batman Begins*. The dark side of Gotham is the underlying theme of the movie, and it could just as well be the subscript of the Night Hotel too.

Gothic Gotham is how the hotel's press release describes the design approach. I would call it Gothic Gotham with a nod to the late David Hicks. The bold, dark colour, the gothic letter 'N' printed on the carpet, the stylized blend of high kitsch, slick Bauhaus modern, and the odd decorative flourish such as a sofa upholstered in pony skin is the kind of striking (Austin Powers style) mix that Hicks was so good at, and obviously the baton has been passed to Mark Zeff of Zeff design.

It's a bold move to choose black as the predominant theme for the interior; you would imagine it would be dark, which it is, and depressing, which surprisingly it is not. Admittedly if you spent a week at the Night and then emerged into daylight you would need some very dark glasses, but otherwise the ambience is a welcoming version of rat-pack cool.

A lot of this has to do with the quality of the approach. Frette linen on the bed, huge flat-screen TVs mounted on the walls (black of course), all the electronic connections a techie could want, plus a bar and restaurant that provide a dark, sexy environment to try inventive fusion finger food such as oriental hot dogs and chili-fried calamari. There's even a mirrored outdoor lounge for the cool New York smokers who refuse to give up, despite the odds.

The true success of Night from a design point of view is the attention to detail. At this hotel, black is decidedly not just black. The walls in the lobby for instance are clad in tiles of custom-made black glass, and the floor is a custom-dyed carpet in a pattern of gothic black-and-white newspaper-style letters. The unspoken rule seems to be, if it's going to be black, let's make it a good black. In Times Square, black is back.

address Night Hotel, 132 West 45th Street, New York, NY 10036
tel +1 (212) 835 9600   **fax** +1 (212) 835 9610
e-mail lbadillo@nighthotelny.com
room rates from $239

absolutely have to see
The Rainbow Grill (30 Rockefeller Plaza, +1 (212) 632 5100) on top of the 'Rock'
(the superb timeless Rockefeller Center) still has the best view of Manhattan
from its legendary sixty-fifth floor bar, restaurant and ballroom.

must have dinner
Just push 'L' in the elevator, turn left in the Night Hotel lobby, and take a seat in
the all-black Night Life restaurant to sample the chef's innovative Asian-inspired
tasting menu. A casual setting for an inventive alternative to finger food.

hotel qt

When André Balazs opened Hotel QT – a former office block off Times Square converted into a design-conscious, luxury version of a YMCA for the Abercrombie & Fitch generation – all the world's press came to have a look. They waxed lyrical about the pool in the lobby, and the reception area that looks like a theatre kiosk, and in the process generated plenty of sound bites like 'Cheap chic magic' and 'Frugal frills with whimsical flair'.

There are newer places opening all the time and by the time I got there, the parade had moved on. Which suited me fine because it only leaves the question: what is left after the hype is over? The answer in the case of Hotel QT is the same as when the hype started. The key to André's success lies in his approach. Long before decisions were made about fabric, furniture, design and décor, he asked the question; how can we make this boring building fun? Thus Hotel QT got its pool. But to say there's a pool in the lobby is not exactly accurate; there's a pool instead of a lobby, just as there is a kiosk – selling all the essentials you need to stock your mini bar – instead of a reception desk. The idea is to forget about traditional expectations. What's the point of a lobby anyway? What do you do there other than wait for your baggage or your wife? Surely it's better to use the space inventively, creating a sensation – a talking point that people are drawn to out of curiosity.

Creating a scene and stimulating curiosity are things Balazs is very good at, a reflection perhaps of his years as a nightclub impresario. The pool, the kiosk, the submerged bar: these are the things that generate attention. Crazy lobby, simple tiny white room is a formula that has worked before in the budget arena.

But in the case of Hotel QT, the rooms are much more than tiny white boxes. Once again, Balazs's signature of innovation and style make the difference. Rather than a plain bed, the guest rooms have leather-upholstered platforms – a much hipper and more practical alternative to silly things like bedheads and night tables. In the bathrooms, a lot of space is saved by avoiding a bath, and wash basins have been replaced by long counter-tops with more than enough space for anyone with a weakness for New York's department-store-sized pharmacies. Given the success of Hotel QT in this new world of hip hotels, perhaps nightclub experience is more important than hotel school.

address Hotel QT, 125 West 45th Street, New York, NY 10036
tel +1 (212) 354 2323 **fax** +1 (212) 302 8585
e-mail info.newyork@hotelqt.com
room rates from $175

absolutely have to see
The American Folk Art Museum (45 West 53rd Street), next to MoMA, takes 'down home' Americana and showcases it in the contrasting monastic monumentality of Tod Williams and Billie Tsien's beautifully designed spaces.

must have lunch
Brasserie (100 East 53rd Street, +1 (212) 751 4840) was remodelled by architects Diller & Scofidio in Mies Van Der Rohe's Seagram Building. With Saarinen chairs and translucent tables, it's a contemporary setting for a contemporary menu.

midtown

Midtown is the centre of Manhattan. The Empire State Building, Grand Central Station, the exquisite beaux-arts beauty of the New York Public Library, Rockefeller Center, the Chrysler Building, Times Square: all the landmarks that define New York can be found in this stretch of Manhattan between 34th and 59th Streets.

Perhaps most dramatically, Midtown is the home of New York's famous 'concrete canyons'. This is where the first modernist 'glass box' – Lever House, a twenty-four-storey building of glass and steel, designed by Gordon Bunshaft – was built, and decades earlier it was here that the race was on to build the biggest and tallest skyscraper in the world. The Chrysler Building won that race, helped by the fact it had a stainless steel spire measuring 121 feet in height placed on top of it. But it held the title only a few months: the Empire State Building, completed in a record 410

days (in one day the 3500 workers managed to add ten storeys), usurped Chrysler's shiny crown. The fact that so many skyscrapers are in Midtown is more than coincidence: Manhattan's bedrock, essential as a stable foundation for such intensive vertical construction, is found mainly in the middle of the island.

With the newly restored Grand Central Station – a result of Jackie Kennedy Onassis's relentless lobbying – the recently completed revamp of MoMA by Japanese architect Yoshio Taniguchi and the arrival of hipper, newer department stores such as Abercrombie & Fitch, Takashimaya, Felissimo and the opening of restaurants such as the Marc Newson-designed Lever House, Midtown is experiencing a revival. And nowhere is this more evident than in the number of funky hotels that have opened in the area, from swanky Chambers to the exotic Dream.

city club hotel

The Harvard Club, the New York Yacht Club, the Penn Club ... the City Club Hotel is located near some of the most famous historic clubs in Manhattan. Proprietor Jeff Klein's mission, when he acquired this property, was to recreate the ambience, the architecture, the style and the atmosphere of what used to be the enclave of New York City's political elite.

The building had good bones: it was once the clubhouse of the City Club of New York, a non-partisan civic association formed in the late 1800s to promote good government. Located on West 44th Street, a stretch of Manhattan that in the early twentieth century was being billed as New York's answer to Pall Mall, the club had a library, a café, a billiard room, a reading room and a dining room, as well as four floors of guest rooms, each with private tub and shower. It was a club on a par with the other fashionable clubs, but sadly the building was sold in 1939. It subsequently suffered the fate of many grand Midtown structures: it became an office building.

In 1999 it was purchased by City Club Hotel (no relation to the club of the same name) and the job commenced to restore a club-like feeling to this stately building. Jeffrey Bilhuber, a designer whose projects include homes for Anna Wintour, Michael Douglas and David Bowie, was brought in to realize Jeff Klein's clearly defined ambition of creating a personal space for sophisticated and discerning guests. Choosing timelessness over invention, the designer opted for a palate of materials such as Honduras mahogany, waxed cork flooring, hand-drawn wallpaper, polished bronze, matte limestone and the odd splash of cashmere and faux fur.

Rich, seductive and aristocratic, the sensuality of the materials mixed with strong original art recreates the style of club that exists in an idealized version of Manhattan. Like Ralph Lauren with his inflated, theatrical perfection of WASP elegance, Bilhuber created a club far more stylish than these clubs ever would have been. Unlike many hotels in New York, the City Club is all about the guest rooms, not the public spaces. These are rooms where you can comfortably and cosily cocoon away from the hubbub of the metropolis. The best part, unlike its neighbours the Harvard Club and the New York Yacht Club, is that you don't need to be a member.

address City Club Hotel, 55 West 44th Street, New York, NY 10036
tel +1 (212) 921 5500 **fax** +1 (212) 944 5544
e-mail info@cityclubhotel.com
room rates from $325

absolutely have to see
The International Center of Photography (1133 Avenue of the Americas at 43rd Street) is an exceptional museum and school established by Cornell Capa, brother of legendary photographer Robert Capa. The permanent collection features all the greats and temporary exhibitits draw on global talents and themes.

must have lunch
DB Bistro Moderne (55 West 44th Street, +1 (212) 391 2400). Be sure to try chef Daniel Boulud's innovative version of the traditional American burger.

morgans

The first time I stayed at Morgans it had just opened. It was the hottest place in town, and the most talked about hotel in the world. Magazines everywhere couldn't get enough of it, and French designer Andrée Putman, who had developed her trade-mark design signature almost by accident – courtesy of divorce and starting all over again – had become a global design super-star, the first, even before Monsieur Starck appeared on the scene. With her distinctive facial profile, asymmetrically styled hair and a black and grey wardrobe to match her interiors, she became an icon of the new design age – almost as recognizable in certain circles as Hitchcock or Churchill.

That's why back in the late 1980s, when the hotel had just launched, and the doors opened, my immediate reaction to sharing an elevator with Andrée Putman was to blurt out 'Hi, how are you?' as if we had been best friends. She just nodded, didn't change one muscle of her facial expression, and darted out of the lift probably thinking 'Oh mon dieu, not another design groupie!' It's hard to imagine twenty-odd years later that there was such a fuss at the time over Morgans black-and-white tiled bathrooms, the monotone colour scheme with the odd Bauhaus lamp and chair. But Morgans was the pioneer, the first hotel to approach its interiors with a design consciousness limited until then to the occasional public architecture project or an exclusive residential commission. Morgans took the notion of decorating a hotel and threw everything out, literally. Before Morgans, the more stuff a hotel managed to shove into a space the more money it could charge. Morgans got rid of the tables, the clocks, the pictures, and all the tchotchkes.

In short, Morgans got rid of the clutter, and in doing so invented a whole new kind of hotel. Thus it was strange to be checking in again two decades later. Would it be a disappointment? Could it still compete with the new crop? The black and grey was gone in the lobby, replaced with red and grey, but not exactly a seismic shift in design. The bedrooms have remained almost the same. Although without doubt there are other more cutting-edge options to choose from in Midtown Manhattan, Morgans has something none of them can match – a proven ability to stand the test of time.

address Morgans, 237 Madison Avenue, New York, NY 10016
tel +1 (212) 686 0300 **fax** +1 (212) 686 0300
e-mail reservationsny@morganshotelgroup.com
room rates from $269

absolutely have to see
The Morgan Library (225 Madison Avenue). It was inevitable that Pierpont Morgan, an original robber baron, would donate his collection of manuscripts, books and drawings to the city of New York. Housed in a neoclassical-style mansion, the Library perfectly epitomizes America's age of elegance.

must have lunch
Head to Russian Samovar (256 West 52nd Street, +1 (212) 757 0168) for vodka, blinis, caviar and borscht after a morning at the Morgan Library.

royalton

The Royalton is a legend. More than any other hotel it's the one that broke the mould – that shook the frumpy hotel world by its overstuffed lapels, and proved that a hotel can be as much fun as a nightclub.

If there were a Grand Prix or World Cup for PR, then in the early 1990s the Royalton would have won it hands down. Ian Schrager and his late partner Steve Rubell (ex Studio 54) set the hotel world alight with their first Midtown hotel Morgans. But that was just a warm-up compared to the frenzy the media world went into when Schrager and Rubell launched their collaboration with the then unknown Philippe Starck. As a hotel, the Royalton has improved tremendously in terms of service and management, and the inventiveness of the design has settled into the new status of a design classic. These days, an indigo blue runner with stylized ghost images that resemble Persian script, wall lamps that look like illuminated rhino horns and white canvas clad wing chairs paired with African tribal stools will not likely get the 'Oh my God I've never seen anything like that' reaction they attracted when the hotel first opened. But Philippe Starck's design solution for a long tunnel-like lobby that fronts 44th as well as 43rd Street is still valid, and it still has enough originality not only to evoke a reaction, but also to compete with the city's crop of new arrivals.

Design, after all, is not fashion – it doesn't exist only for the moment, driven by the insane need for constant change. The Royalton's white hot days are over, and you might not find Anna Wintour having lunch or Graydon Carter planning his next issue of *Vanity Fair* over a cocktail. But how important is that anyway?

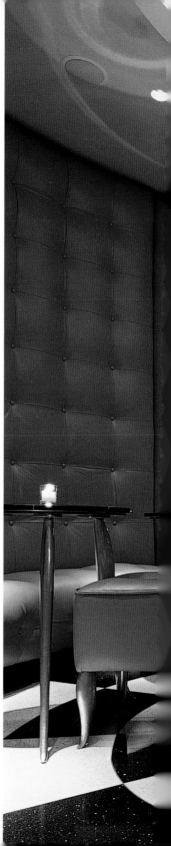

The Royalton is no longer a 'scene', and some say thank God for that. At least you can finally get a table at Forty Four without having to know someone, or a drink in the lobby without having to shop at Dolce & Gabbana first. Starck's design has lasted remarkably well. In fact I hope they don't change it because it still works, and the rooms, particularly those with fireplaces, are still amongst the most spacious and innovative, even compared with New York's new crop of hotels. The only criticism I have is the same criticism I had almost two decades ago – the place is dark. But dark is back in, and compared to the new Night Hotel, it's not dark at all. The Royalton remains the Starck project that launched all the other Starck projects. It is an important piece of design, and hopefully it will be allowed to stay as such.

address Royalton, 44 West 44th Street, New York, NY 10036
tel +1 (212) 869 4400 **fax** +1 (212) 869 4400
e-mail reservationsny@morganshotelgroup.com
room rates from $269

absolutely have to see
Grand Central Station (East 42nd Street and Park Avenue) looks more like a museum than a station, and with cocktail bars like the quirky Campbell Apartment set in a former trustee's office, there's more to do than just wander around.

must have lunch
Grand Central Oyster Bar (+1 (212) 490 6650). Following a renovation spearheaded by the late Jackie Kennedy Onassis, Grand Central is back to its pre-war beauty and the Oyster Bar is once again a favourite lunch spot for the city's suits.

library hotel

Books, books and more books. It's an appropriate theme for a hotel situated on Library Way – the nickname for the stretch of 41st Street that leads to the New York Public Library and is paved at regular intervals with bronze plaques inscribed with quotations from some of the world's most acclaimed writers.

The Library is not the first hotel to offer a library on the premises, or to use books as a decorative ingredient, but it's certainly the first to base itself entirely on books. The small lobby, accordingly, is framed by bookshelves, and the reception desk is designed as a faux card catalogue that could once have housed library index cards. The second floor lounge, the place where breakfast is served, is similarly lined in bookcases that also serve as handy dividers for the seating arrangements.

But the bibliophile approach doesn't stop there. The rooftop bar, a beautiful space that could double as Cary Grant's penthouse in a stylish pre-war New York film, is called Bookmarks, and comprises the dark, moody area known as the Writer's Den, (complete with fireplace) and the Poetry Garden, as well as the outside terraces.

But surely the most distinctive extravagance of all is to classify the guest rooms using the traditional library classification code of the Dewey Decimal System, so that there are no room numbers or names, just book categories. For instance, the fourth floor is classified as Languages, and my room was labelled 400.006. Ancient Languages. This is no mere gimmick: all the books inside the guest rooms are specific to their individual category. Hence in my room, the shelves were full of books on ... ancient languages.

It certainly makes a change from all the same magazines most New York hotels place in their rooms. And how can a consistent association with books be anything but rewarding? The Library is a cosy, clubby hotel within spitting distance (if you're a strong spitter) of the New York Public Library, as well as Grand Central Station.

address Library Hotel, 299 Madison Avenue at 41st Street, New York, NY 10017
tel +1 (212) 983 4500 **fax** +1 (212) 499 9099
e-mail reservations@libraryhotel.com
room rates from $345

absolutely have to see
New York Public Library (Fifth Avenue between 40th and 42nd Streets) is the most impressive beaux-arts building in New York, with items of special interest such as the desk of Charles Dickens and the enormous coffered 630-seat reading room where Trotsky worked just before the Russian Revolution.

must have lunch
On a nice day head to Bryant Park Grill (+1 (212) 840 6500) behind the Library, where you can lunch or dine in a completely unexpected outdoor restaurant.

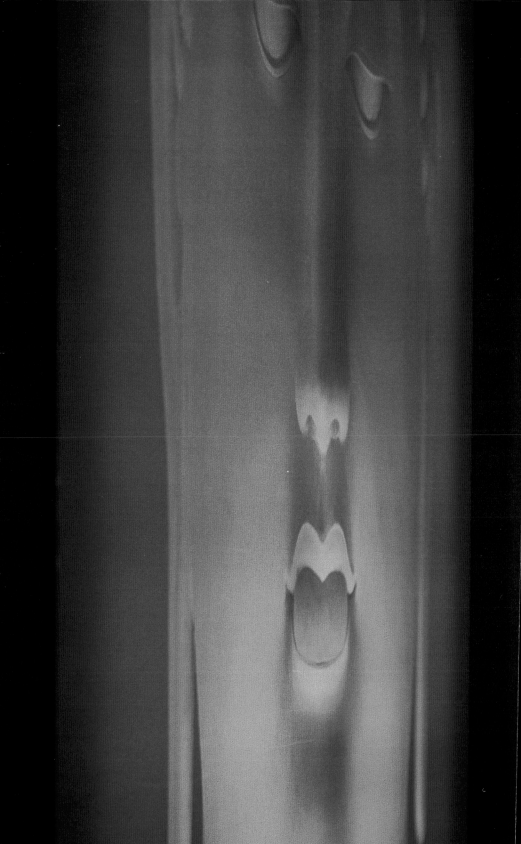

dream

Opened in 2004 on 55th Street and Broadway, Dream is the fourth hotel from actor and entrepreneur Vikram Chatwal. Dubbed the 'turbaned cowboy' by New York media, Chatwal is developing a string of hotels where imagination is on an equal level with service.

Perhaps redeveloping is a more accurate description. With imagination as his operating mantra, he has worked wonders with the Hampshire Hotels and Resorts that his father systematically acquired all around New York over the years. Dream is an apt title for this hotel, because it surely describes the life of this family. The story starts with Sant Chatwal, an Indian Air Force fighter pilot who decided after retiring from service to move to Ethiopia to teach English. Once established there, he started experimenting with catering and opened an Indian restaurant. When Emperor Haile Selassie was deposed, the Chatwals moved to Canada and eventually settled in New York, where Chatwal opened the now legendary Bombay Palace, the first restaurant to offer a five star version of Indian cuisine. It was an instant success, and within three years there was a chain of Bombay Palaces in five different countries.

It's a far cry from Ethiopia to the cover of Asian *Forbes* (on which Vikram Chatwal has just featured), and surely this is the quintessential American dream. But Vikram Chatwal had a more surreal definition in mind when he commenced the overhaul of the former Majestic. That's how a suspended crystal galleon, a monumental copper statue of Catherine the Great in Mongolian clothes, and the largest tropical fish tank in the northern hemisphere ended up being together in one place.

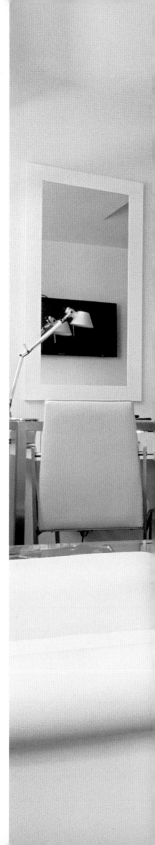

But most unexpected perhaps in the menu of contributors is Deepak Chopra, with his wellness centre one floor down from the lobby. This centre is Deepak Chopra's New York headquarters, not just a handy licensing arrangement, and the treatments on offer are effective and authentic. On top of the building, at the other end of the dosha scale, is Dream's Ava bar, another rooftop venue to join Manhattan's current infatuation with roofbars. Ava, it has to be said, has a visual edge with one of the best views of Times Square anywhere in New York. Dream was conceived by Vikram Chatwal to facilitate dreams, and the hotel's slogan, 'You provide the dream, we provide the service' says it all.

address Dream, 210 West 55th Street, New York, NY 10019
tel +1 (212) 247 2000 **fax** +1 (646) 756 2088
e-mail mtesta@dreamny.com
room rates from $275

absolutely have to see
The extraordinary view of Times Square from Ava, the rooftop bar in Dream, is the best and most comprehensive perspective of the bright lights of Broadway.

must have lunch
It seems strange to suggest a meal in an area called Hell's Kitchen, but the Trattoria dell'Arte (+1 (212) 245 9800) on 900 Seventh Avenue between 56th and 57th Streets is a tasteful and affordable venue for classic Italian food, frequented by the fashionable crowd you would not have found in New York a few years ago.

chambers

A tony address with a downtown mentality – Chambers is a new kind of uptown hotel. The art consciousness that one would expect from SoHo or TriBeCa has been mixed with the more formal, well-dressed profile of a Fifth Avenue address. Situated a stone's throw away from Fifth Avenue's most glamorous boutiques, Chambers is in one of the most desirable Midtown areas, just below Central Park.

At first glance, the interior, an eclectic mix of tribal stools, velvet-clad contemporary design and serious art, seems out of place in a neighbourhood normally more comfortable with imitation French grandeur, and that's its strength. Chambers is an oasis for people who need to be uptown, but whose aesthetic and lifestyle is more downtown. Architect David Rockwell, a veteran of some very famous restaurant installations, was brought in to realize an interior to go with the art. For many hotels, art is an afterthought, simply something to put on the walls. At Chambers, art was the starting point. The proprietors of the hotel are serious collectors, and the property was intended as a rotating showcase for their substantial collection. Larger works hang in the public spaces, smaller ones are featured in the guest rooms. I admit I have always been a bit sceptical of the hotel as a gallery, but at Chambers it works because it reflects a genuine and intelligently conceived collection, and one that is, as with some of New York's top smaller museums, constantly changing. During my stay, the collection consisted of contemporary artists from Asia: a fascinating mix of photography, painting, works on paper and sculpture, the likes of which you would normally not find in one place.

With raw concrete ceilings, industrial lamps bolted to the walls, polished concrete bathroom floors and drafting table-style trestle work tops complete with steel vintage work stools, the interiors are not what you would expect from a hotel around the corner from Tiffany's. But that's exactly why it works – a bit of edge between the poodles and the Bentleys is a good thing.

address Chambers, 15 West 56th Street, New York, NY 10019
tel +1 (212) 974 5656 **fax** +1 (212) 974 5657
e-mail reservations@chambershotel.com
room rates from $350

absolutely have to see
Lever House (390 Park Avenue at 53rd Street) is New York's first modernist skyscraper, and a pioneer of steel-frame glass-clad architecture.

must have lunch
Lever House Restaurant (+1 (212) 888 2700), Lever House, by now almost as famous as its host building, is a funky contemporary cocoon courtesy of design rockstar Marc Newson, with a cuisine that makes it one of the most talked-about restaurants in Manhattan.

upper east side

North of 59th Street and east of Central Park, the Upper East Side is the patrician neighbourhood of Manhattan. A two square mile grid that includes famous Fifth, Madison and Park Avenues, this is where in the late 1800s and early 1900s the Vanderbilts, the Carnegies, the Rockefellers, the Astors and the Whitneys built elaborate mansions, a cross between a French townhouse and a British baronial pile. Inspired by the grand homes in the Old World, these families mimicked the lifestyle and architecture of landed aristocracy in Europe, and in the process created a fashion for a neoclassical bonanza of marble parquetry and panelling. They were the grandees, whose impetus to move this far north in the city is often credited to Mrs Astor. She couldn't bear that her son built the Waldorf Astoria immediately next door to her residence, and so off she set to live by the (newly completed) Central Park.

RAPHAEL
at the Met

The Upper East Side remains the residential quarter of many of Manhattan's movers and shakers. Because of constantly rising property prices, a few mansions have been replaced by even larger apartment buildings. But thankfully, a few of these townhouses survived, largely because some of them were given to the city – complete with their magnificent art collections – to function thereafter as museums. Hence the nickname 'Museum Mile' – the greatest concentration of museums in the world. The Frick, the Guggenheim, the Cooper-Hewitt, the Whitney, the National Academy, the Neue Galerie and of course the Met, are all near to each other. Lucky for New York that the disparagingly nicknamed robber barons collected art, and even luckier that it was acceptable for one generation to dedicate their lives to making money, and for the next to dedicate theirs to giving it away.

the carlyle

I used to stay at The Mark and my girlfriend used to stay at The Carlyle. It was classic odd couple stuff. I would try to convince her how The Mark was smaller, quieter and more sophisticated; she was convinced by the history and elegance of The Carlyle, not to mention the fact that the hotel was largely made up of permanent residents. In the end, she was right. The Carlyle's continuing ability to stay completely true to itself, irrespective of fashion or trend, has made it one of New York's most genuine and charismatic experiences.

Nightclub entertainer Bobby Short played live in the Café Carlyle every week until shortly before his death, and Woody Allen can often be found jamming with his clarinet in the very same café on a Monday night. On the design front, the hotel had not touched the original scheme by legendary pre-war decorator Dorothy Draper until recently. Even when they did, they cleverly chose architect Thierry Despont for the task, placing trust in his well-publicized taste and preference for respect of authenticity and continuity.

Perhaps the most convincing quality of The Carlyle is how in sync it is with the area. The Carlyle is the Upper East Side, and vice versa. All the values of patrician New York – a resistance to change, unyielding embrace of quality together with a certain 'hauteur' – are the qualities that define The Carlyle. This doesn't make it everyone's cup of tea, but then the hotel is not trying to be. People who are not fans of the Upper East Side might describe it as boring, but how can a neighbourhood that has a world class museum on practically every other corner, not to mention the proximity of Central Park, possibly be boring?

The Upper East Side is interesting precisely because it's not like the rest of New York. The doormen with their traditional brass-buttoned coats and caps, school children in blazers and ties, discreet little restaurants tucked into the brownstones on gentrified side streets, and, of course, the shopping, all give this part of New York a signature as distinctive as the tenement housing of the Lower East Side. Originally built in 1930, designed by the architectural firm of Bien & Prince, The Carlyle was intended as a residential hotel and has remained as such ever since. It has featured in countless films set in Manhattan, and its pervasive sense of refinement continues to be a magnet. It may not be everyone's idea of the real New York, but it is a hotel that will make a stay in Manhattan a truly memorable experience.

address The Carlyle, 35 East 76th Street, New York, NY 10021
tel +1 (212) 744 1600 **fax** +1 (212) 717 4682
e-mail thecarlyle@rosewoodhotels.com
room rates from $550

absolutely have to see
The Frick Collection (1 East 70th Street) is set in the former residence of Henry Clay Frick, a railroad tycoon whose art collection is displayed in an entirely domestic context. This is a brilliantly directed approach to exhibiting timeless art.

must have lunch
You're on Museum Mile. So why not lunch at Bid Brasserie (1334 York Avenue at 71st Street, +1 (212) 988 7730), the Dineen Nealy designed restaurant in Sotheby's? After breakfast at Tiffany's, there's lunch at Sotheby's.

upper west side

THEODOR

In the early 1800s the area north of what is now 59th Street was still a wilderness of wooded hills and valleys and the odd shantytown. Building didn't really start in earnest until the latter part of the nineteenth century when a boom was stimulated by the extension of the subway to the north of the island. With the completion of Central Park imminent – an 840-acre eden of several lakes and several million trees, which had taken more than twenty years to bring to conclusion – the established money families had started to decamp further north to the Upper East Side. From a development point of view, it was only natural to assume that the other side of the park would be even more desirable because it would have the benefit of the rising sun. The buildings planned for what would become the Upper West Side were the grandest New York had ever seen for residential purposes.

The Dakota, completed in 1884, kicked off the trend. New Yorkers at the time couldn't help but snipe that the building was so far away that it might as well be in Dakota. The developers obviously had a sense of humour, because the name stuck – chiselled in stone on the building's façade. The trend was set. The Dakota marked the beginning of the Upper West Side, and the beginning of the rivalry between the two sides of the park. Residents west of the Greensward Plan (the original name of the park) dismissed the Upper East Side crowd as inbred snobs, and the Park Avenue crowd in turn thought of the other side of the park as home to upper middle-class libertines. And so it has remained ever since.

hudson

When the Hudson first opened it created quite a buzz. Not because it was another innovative Starck–Schrager co-production, but more because it was an *affordable* Starck–Schrager co-production. More unlikely still, an affordable hotel with 1000 rooms; 'boutique' had just become 'department store'.

The Hudson was exactly what New York needed – the city is always short of hotel rooms. The idea behind the pricing was as unconventional as Starck's design. The rooms would be charged according to availability and demand. You could end up paying $95, $160, $210, $260 or more, for the same room depending entirely on when you booked it.

A HIP HOTEL a stone's throw from Central Park on New York's Upper West Side, with affordable rates and plenty of rooms – it seemed too good to be true, and indeed there was one small catch. The rooms are small – small enough to generate lots of anecdotes. When I checked in, the girl behind the reception desk – which must rank as one of the longest reception desks in the world – handed me the key and announced, 'Here you are, you have a deluxe queen double.' 'Thank you,' I replied. Into the elevator I went, straight to my room, opened the door and realized there must be a mistake. The room was beautiful, but tiny. Just enough space for a queen-size bed, a few closets, a little desk, a flat-screen TV and a very small bathroom. In short, everything you could need from a New York bolthole, but surely this was not a deluxe queen double. Back down I went to reception. 'I think there's a mistake,' I announced. The receptionist checked and replied, 'No sir, you're in a deluxe queen double.' 'That's impossible, how can a non-deluxe queen be any smaller?'

'It's not a matter of size,' she explained to me. 'It's a matter of height. The higher the floor, the higher the rating, the more expensive the room.'

On reflection, all of this is quite smart. A bit like Henry Ford: any colour you want as long as it's black. Life without too many choices is nice and simple. In any case, the Hudson was designed to encourage you not to be in your room. With a series of bars and restaurants that still rank among the busiest in the city, the idea is to use your room only to crash. It's a valid strategy. How much easier it is to just take an elevator downstairs and choose between the Hudson Cafeteria, Library Bar, Hudson Bar, Sky Terrace and Private Park, rather than head off in a taxi and have to find your way home late at night. And when you do finally push the elevator button to go back up, it's quite reassuring to know that no one in the hotel has a bigger room than you.

address Hudson, 356 West 58th Street, New York, NY 10019
tel +1 (212) 554 6000   **fax** +1 (212) 554 6001
e-mail reservationsny@morganshotelgroup.com
room rates from $209

absolutely have to see
Lincoln Center for the Performing Arts (140 West 65th Street). The East Side has the Met, the West Side has the Lincoln Center: New York's hub for music, ballet and opera. The architecture amplifies the visual impact of the performing arts.

must have dinner
Café Des Artistes (1 West 67th Street, +1 (212) 877 3500). Decorated with Howard Chandler Christy's mural of naughty nude nymphs, this discreetly hidden bistro is the perfect venue for a pre- or post-Lincoln Center performance.

HIP® HOTELS and HIP HOTELS® are the registered trademarks of
Hip Hotels Media Ltd. All rights are reserved.

© 2006 Hip Hotels Media Ltd

First published in 2006 in paperback in the United States of America by
Thames & Hudson Inc., 500 Fifth Avenue, New York, New York 10110

thamesandhudsonusa.com

Library of Congress Catalog Card Number 2005910938

ISBN-13:   978-0-500-28618-0
ISBN-10:   0-500-28618-3

Printed and bound in Singapore by CS Graphics

Designed by Maggi Smith